YOU LEAD, YOU FOLLOW

You Lead, You Follow

Making all the right moves
in the corporate world!

Robin E Silas BSA, MSA

iUniverse, Inc.
NewYork Bloomington

You Lead, You Follow
Making all the right moves in the corporate world!

iUniverse books may be ordered through booksellers or by contacting:

iUniverse
1663 Liberty Drive
Bloomington, IN 47403
www.iuniverse.com
1-800-Authors (1-800-288-4677)

Because of the dynamic nature of the Internet, any Web addresses or links contained in this book may have changed since publication and may no longer be valid.

ISBN: 978-1-4502-0629-7 (sc)
ISBN: 978-1-4502-0630-3 (ebk)

Printed in the United States of America

iUniverse rev. date: 4/5/2010

Contents

Chapter One
Mark your territory

Do not be fooled into thinking there is no such thing as corporate culture. It exists, and it always will. It will live on as long as human nature exists. Know that it is real and that you must not only accept its presence, but respect it as well. The corporate culture is the most powerful invisible force that controls the decision making process of every single person in the corporation. Master the art of wielding the culture and it will immortalize you.

To me the corporate culture are the "rules" that are the governing guidelines of any organization. "Do this, but not this," and so on. They are never really explicitly explained; they are perceived by individuals. Here is question number one: Is your interpretation of what is happening the same as the person next to you, or even the same as everyone else in the room? Do not rely on your own interpretation of events and body language to determine corporate culture: clarify by dialogue, not chit-chat.

Dialogue is actual conversation. It involves give and take, input, output, and most importantly, feedback. Once you have clearly identified what the cultural norms are, you will need to practice them!

I remember studying a math book that my parents gave me when I was in grade school to help polish my skills during the summer months. There was a small owl on almost every other page that declared, "Practice makes perfect!" We have all heard this, but we keep forgetting to implement this pattern into our lives. We must learn the rules and practice them to better understand why they are in place and their root interpretations.

Once you have lived within the corporate culture and you breathe the very mission statement into your veins, you are ready to make your move.

All business professionals, no matter how adept, have areas where performance can be improved. You will not be successful anywhere unless you create corporate habits that will give you the frame of reference you need to succeed. Remember to be humble. Regardless of your position you can still be a change agent. You can be a leader.

Chapter Two
The red herring effect

There is a fish known as a red herring. It has a tremendous scent that is so strong it is used to train pursuit dogs. In basic terms, dogs are given a scent to pursue in an exercise, and in between the start and finish line a red herring fish is thrown into the mix. Its purpose is to cancel the memory and pursuit of the original scent. It is there solely to throw off the lead. Only the dogs that are able to overcome the test of the red herring and successfully regain the original scent are graduates of the program.

You need a red herring in your reserve bank. There are those within any corporation who are there to specifically exploit your weaknesses for their professional resume. You must plan to have a red herring that can be placed right in the path of those who want to push you out the door.

How can this be done? The key is information. There are internal grapevines, and then there are the external grapevines. You want to know who is who and what is up. Get in on the external grapevine channel, where the broadcasts are always in high definition. A key to gathering data is how you process that data; just because you are aware of something doesn't mean you use it to your advantage. External grapevines can be very damaging to a corporation as anything in life that is abused. Use this data carefully and under the common theme of what is best for your career and the corporation. If those two issues don't blend together, find a new job. Once you have that data such as employer cultural values, change agents, or moles, base a plan of protection or attack; then test it out. Is someone really a mole in the corporation? Are you sure they will betray your trust? Send out a little harmless piece of data and see how it plays out. One of the biggest mistakes we make is taking everything at face value. Stop that right away. Don't react to everything as if it were true; most of the time it is not! Again, get the data, process it, and test it out. Once you know that you have some good resources, plan your career with some body armor for protection.

You must be able to protect yourself within a corporation, period.

We must understand the nature of man. Moral laws are being operated in the realm of grey for years; corruption is running rampant.

The World War Two generation had it the best. Even marriages at that time were about two people coming together to face the brave new world.

Hand shakes and a firm yes are meaningless today. Do you really think you are going to get hired, do a good job, get fair pay, and work there for the next forty years and then retire? Wake up!

We are living in a self-centered world where the ultimate goal is power and money. The amazing part is that without relationships there is no power. What power does the CEO of a major corporation have if there are no employees?

My lesson in this chapter is that you must respect the relationship you have to the corporation as a whole, and protect this relationship. Get involved with the external grapevine and get the facts. Only then can you stand alone in a time of necessity.

Remember that you can only control yourself. Be prepared at all times.

Chapter Three

Your life is an orange peel

Yes you are nothing more than an orange peel. There is a school of thought that everyone is made up of three layers. The core is your deepest values. This is what your parents have given you. Had a hard life or absent parental figure? Well, you got some work to do—respect your weaknesses and lack of personal experience. You won't learn anything unless you are open to it. On top of this layer is our self-esteem, what we really think about ourselves. Then our last level is our public image, what we want people to see, your orange peel.

You must accept as I have that we are not perfect. We can't get everything we want in life, and we need to first be happy with who we are and what we have right now. Only then will we be happy with our gains, no matter the size of the gain.

Now, in corporate mediums public image is key. But that is not the end-all-be-all. People only show what they think you want to see or what they want to show you, not what they are truly about. To get past the orange peel, you must have some level of commonness and trust between each other. Also you must value the relationship enough to want to preserve it in its current state.

Want to really know your boss and what makes them tick? Don't respond to all the signals sent from someone's orange peel. If you do they will only continue to send them to you, create a link between the two of you by means of self-esteem or core values to really dig deeper and position yourself with them on a personal level.

Get past the orange peel and you will be better off longevity-wise within the corporation. People are less likely to sabotage or fire someone they have been personally intimate with on a conciseness level.

Ever get into a fight? There are ever forged realms that will always be in effect.

Topic of discussion
Your personal thoughts and feelings
The relationship

When you engage in an argument with someone, these three processes are in motion. You will of course be focused on the first two in the beginning, but at some point you must come to the acceptance that the relationship is most important. This will give you the process to reach an agreement that is a win-win. Without having the passion in your heart about the relationship, you will promote the first two areas of engagement to either get what you want, with serious consequences to the relationship, or there will no longer be a relationship.

Do you care about your boss enough to invest time to get past their orange peel? Are you passionate enough about your relationships at work to value them in times of disagreement?

Answer these questions honestly and you won't waste your time. Therefore, you need to be in a place of employment where you value that place and the relationships you have there. It has been documented that a happy employee will not be lost to a competitor regardless of compensation differences if that employee is happy. And with us spending more time at work than anywhere else, why not be happy?!

Chapter Four

Never use cruise control

The day you set your career on auto pilot is the day you hit the big red self destruct button. Never be comfortable, but don't go nuts. The word is balanced. Like in nature when things get out of balance, things go out of control.

Stress is a major human evil that is built into us. There is nothing right about stress. You must learn self-control to be a survivor and leader in a corporation. No one will listen to a stressed-out leader.

How do you keep you stress under control? Self-discipline. It's not one act that is going to help you control stress; it is a slippery-slope. Adding one part on another until there are no visible parts, only the one lean machine.

Go to bed at a good time, eat a good balance of meals, work out two to three times a week, have a personal life, read a good book (like this one!) and laugh about something once a day. Whatever you do never slack off, never feel like you don't need to work at something anymore, because then you'll lose it.

Married or in a relationship? Keep on telling your partner that you value them, that they are important to you. Go to work and let them see your optimistic personality. Everyone needs hope, but many are not prepared to do the work it takes to keep hope alive. One way to really stand out in the workplace is to be positive about outcomes and the vision of the corporate goals.

People today are drawn to positive thinking people, because they are happy and successful. And I am not talking just about financial statements. Success is not just about your paycheck, and anyone who is truly happy is not just a millionaire. It's a state of mind, people. Stay hungry, stay focused, and keep the passion burning.

If you don't have the drive, no one is going to want to be a passenger. Get your edge by simply having the right attitude. We all hear about how positive emotional energy is important for people that have had traumatic experiences such as cancer surgery or auto accidents to recover. Stress is a silent killer—it works its poison over time, and it is nothing but negative energy. Everyone today needs to feel good, and not just put on a happy face; that will not work nor last for too long. Let your work environment be a place that will fuel your positive energy toward the rest of your personal life, instead of vice versa. Why keep leaving the house each day hating your job or boss and coming home venting about it?! It's just never-ending negativity that will make you a total loser in life. Stop it. Get your edge by having the right attitude for success that will not let you settle for the everyday routines because you care about what you are doing and where you work.

Chapter Five

You want it, come get it

I learned a lesson at the tender age of eighteen years that stuck with me ever since. If you make a mistake at your job, accept the blame.

Too many people are too quick to point the finger at someone else or circumstantial details. You make a mistake, it is your fault!! Be responsible for your actions, or you won't be respected and you will never be an effective leader. Bosses will actually trust someone more who is honest enough to say that they are at fault and are willing to work at fixing it and never repeating the mistake again. Doesn't that make sense?

Got a problem at work? Here is the master plan—come up with at least three solutions that may work and pitch them to your boss or at the next board meeting. None of them may work out but at least you are trying, and maybe they will lead to a great solution. Don't just complain about something with no plan of attack.

I remember a situation once in a board room meeting where one of the directors yelled out, "We are all just peas in a barrel rolling around and around!" Things can get very frustrating in your office, but someone has to be a hero. Be in control. It is a weaker employee who loses control and gets angry. The one with patience is the stronger one. If you want to climb the corporate ladder, you need to be in control, and that means not being angry all the time. Be firm but not disrespectful about your views. People within the office, regardless of their position, all make it move in the direction it needs to go in. Everyone needs to feel valuable and respected.

It takes a strong person to accept that they are wrong. If you desire to better yourself, explore the world of responsibility. Only then can you truly be ready to lead others. It is not easy to be a leader. The opportunities to operate in an unethical or illegal manner are not only more often but easier to execute. You must be able to have a clear conscience, to be able to do what is right even when you are totally alone.

True character development occurs when you are in a struggle. Don't run away from problems. Face them. It's only within life's struggles that we mature and learn.

And when those times come into our lives, remember it is better to make a mistake and learn from it than to avoid the problem and live in fear. Be confident in yourself, and others will have confidence in you.

Remember in the last chapter about positive energy and the right attitude? It's negative to sit in a meeting and defend your position when you know you are wrong. Also, it makes your employer's job harder in that they have to stress out about talking to you. I hope you can see how this force is useless and pointless. Think I am crazy? Go ask your boss if they had something negative they needed to tell you but knew that you would be fine with it and would accept your blame as needed if that would make them feel easier about being honest with you about your job performance ... told you I was right.

Now is the time to be accountable for your actions. This book is not designed to pamper your emotions; its purpose is to give you what you need.

Chapter Six

Break dance verses disco

Break dancing and disco, while different in style, are symbols of popular dance in the past few decades. And those who mastered the moves became the spotlight owners of clubs, schools, and media. It is so interesting how people underestimate body language in communication.

On the phone a person's tone of voice is the most dominating communication signal, but face to face it is our body language that makes or breaks us. During a rehearsal for your meeting or perhaps new interview, how many of us go over our body language? Enter a room and own it with your demeanor. Trust me, everyone will know you are someone important regardless of your position.

It is also a great positional tool for you. Proper body language is important in having others in your corporation believe your ideas are sound and valid.

Reflect on someone whom you admire. Does that person exhibit excellent body language? Of course they do! You let people know where you stand on a topic without saying a word.

This can be a positive or negative message. But you must learn what type of beat is playing in your corporation. Ever try doing the moonwalk to heavy metal music? Not only does it not fit, but you look like a total fool.

Now let's talk about a dancing partner.

I recall the horrific story of a family in Kansas that were brutally murdered by two men, who had no individual criminal behaviors in their past. A medical review of the two men produced interesting results. The first male was interviewed individually and was quiet, nonaggressive, and was deemed unable to administer and execute such an evil act.

Now the second male was interviewed alone. He was funny, polite, and also was deemed unable to hurt a family in such a manner. So the medical review forwarded to bringing both men in together. In minutes the two men together became a force of evil, which clearly demonstrates the power of relationships and the importance of your team players.

Ever think that another coworker would be a better teammate for you? Or that a different boss would make you a better employee? You never know how bad things could be with a new partnership in the office. Never assume that a change within a corporation will work based on corporate friendly relationships. Eating lunch together is not working together. Putting two people together could be a great success or a total disaster.

You may be in the best situation you could have in your current job and relationships. Never underestimate your current settings, and always try to excel no matter what the conditions. If things don't work out in your position or with a coworker or supervisor, a change will only support your drive toward your professional goals.

Remember that you could be in the best place at the right time, right now.

Chapter Seven
Who talk you how to spoke?

Today I find it surprising how little detail is given to orientation and consistent scheduled meetings. And how these scheduled meetings are conducted, to the point where most people walk away disenchanted. If you want to be an effective leader and have a polished presentation, you must possess the means of captivating your audience for a short period of time with an opportunity for feedback.

Communication is complex; the main parts are the channel and message. In marketing, people are always thinking creatively, but in reality, you are simply placing a message on a pre-established channel. It's for retention value that you want the message to stick. It's the same in a meeting presentation. Let people walk away with something to talk about and remember. And don't make it a laundry list of items, just a few things.

In a meeting follow the body language, and remember people will more likely stay focused if you keep glancing at them throughout your presentation.

Remember people already know how to communicate with each other, but frame of reference is very important.

I remember a critical thinking exercise from Central Michigan University where there was this fictional story. I don't remember the names so I will add them in.

A woman called "Angela" wanted to get across a river to her boyfriend "Don." She was not able to swim across and needed a boat. She found a ship with a captain named "Jim," who heard her desire and offered an exchange. He would take her across the river if she had an intimate night with him. She was shocked and went to her friend named "Iris." Iris told her that she would not give her any direction and it was up to Angela what she wanted to do. Days went by and finally Angela agreed and fulfilled Jim's price. Jim then honored his agreement and took her across the river. She then went to Don, who asked how she got across. When Angela told him, he was very upset and told her to leave and never return. Upset and crying, Angela walked away and after a long walk sat down on a park bench. There a young man named "Ivan" found her depressed and alone. He asked what had happened, and after hearing her story, Ivan stormed away to find Jim and then pummeled him into the earth.

Now the exercise asked for each student to rank the characters in the story from one to five, one representing the best person and five the worst. Here is a brief outline of which state rated some of the characters at number one.

- Michigan – Iris (stay out of it)
- Texas – Ivan (cowboy to the rescue)
- New York – Jim (we got a deal)
- Utah – Angela (symbolized self sacrifice)

Each state has its own culture and religious values. We must appreciate each person, and that they bring different interpretations of the same message. Remember that when you are describing something to another person, clarify by means of feedback that they understand what you are explaining according to your interpretation not theirs.

Frame of reference is very important to hold in your forefront. State your message, repeat it, and then have it repeated back to you. Don't let people make decisions of your ideas that they totally don't see through your eyes.

Remember, my apple looks totally different than yours; unless you were envisioning a red cartoon apple with a smiling worm coming out if it.

Therefore, communication from body language to ensuring that you are interpreting what someone is saying to you in their eyes is extremely important. People are all different, with different ideas about how to do the exact same thing. Respect that and take time to make sure your ideas are communicated effectively to the other person. This means that they see what you see. Get some feedback or draw a picture whatever it takes to get you there!

Chapter Eight
The cost of ethics

Relationships are so important today in our society, and yet we operate as if they don't exist. Our generation is too focused on what we want, and not on what is best for the organization. We must respect the needs of the corporation, and not our personal feelings about issues.

This concept is true about ethics. Some people are driven by their moral compass and others by their personal feelings. Your personal feelings will always drive you to achieve perceived happiness, regardless of the cost. Your moral compass will always lead you to the right decision, the ethical and legal answer - which may not make you happy, but is the right decision nonetheless.

Mold your thoughts into this process. As you move up the corporate ladder, you will be faced with more decisions that reflect your character and mold your professional path.

You may have the power to decide if someone is hired, fired, given a raise or disciplined. These decisions will be based on your personal character traits. This is why it is important to know what your self core values are, and to improve on them.

People will respond to your personality and anticipate your moves. This is in essence your influence on the corporate culture. If you operate in a way that gives people the impression that you are fair and responsible, then they will also make decisions in that manner. Others, regardless of whether they are good or evil in their intentions, will operate around you in that manner and so on. Let your decisions reflect how you would want others to perform.

And if you can accomplish this, then you are one step closer to the hardest part of leadership—let go. Employers today are too quick to make every decision in a micromanagement process. This is utterly useless and will only lead to a total breakdown in the corporation or the employer. Empower the employees to make decisions and trust in them, then they will respect you and trust you. Employers should not assume that the employees must demonstrate trust and loyalty first; it should be by the corporation first, reciprocated by the employee.

I remember an event in a small town years ago when the company (A) was facing a tough few months due to supply shortages. The company was one of three of the same supply companies in the same town. The other two companies laid off employees with no pay for four months. Company (A) decided to do something more about the company as a whole, laid off everyone but paid them in full for the four months. In return the staff were to polish up on their performance and education. When the business supply returned all three companies reopened to full production, but company (A) out-performed the other two, and got a lot more business due to the fact that management was beyond ethical, not to mention that the entire town wanted to only work for them! That is the type of business you want to work for, buy from and respect.

You must clearly think things through every decision you make as an employee. Remember: a decision to not make a decision is also a decision!

Your position in the company is more than a figure, your decisions will lead to fame or disaster, and no employer will release an effective employee. If you are truly good at what you do, your salary will not be an issue, because people will be fighting over you, which means financial security.

Work hard and keep fighting. You'll win no matter the odds. You will win.

Chapter Nine

Perception on reflection

Remember everything I wrote about earlier. Perception is everything in our corporate world. To be a winner you have to believe you are one. This is a critical skill set that you must have and rehearse over and over until it is part of your nature.

This is the foundation you need in order to move to the next level. I remember a meeting I had with a marketing firm that was aiding me with marketing theory in general. One of the most valuable terms that they gave me was to be of the same mind-set as the leaders of my industry. You like someone, think like them, and you will become them.

It's like if you surround yourself with people that are negative, then you will be negative. If you are surrounded by people that have no goals and are not heading in any direction, neither will you. You need to find people that are winners and surround yourself with them. Only then will you believe in the possibilities.

I would frequently go on weekends and visit open houses. However I would only go to those in rich areas, you know those multi-million dollar homes! Anyway, to walk into one of them is awesome, to see the layout and the whole presence of them.

I would constantly think, *Why can I not get here one day?* These are not people that have some special skill set that I don't have or are only here due to privilege. Anyone can own a million-dollar home. If you have not visited one of these homes, go this weekend. You can have it all just like anyone else, just have the perception that you can have it.

I always read about taking baby steps, but that is not my way. You might get too wrapped up into details and lose focus on the main goal that you have. You are no less than anyone else; no one is better than you. Believe this today.

Walk out your door and have a new attitude, one where you will only be living where you are for the next year only. You will increase your pay in six months, and you will have a balanced life.

There is no pick and choose, some bargaining that you can angle into this. It is all or nothing. All or nothing, all or nothing, all or nothing, get what I am saying?

Remember it is not like you need a new job in six months. Start a small personal business out of your apartment or home. Do something that will move you toward your goals, every single day.

Perception is paramount—without it no plan of yours will work. Change your perception on things by simply having the right attitude as we have discussed before; it's not a simple "I am going to be happy." You need to work at this and be committed. Remember a balanced life of personal, business, and healthy living standards with real core values and expectations. Polish your perception skills each day by being aware of them, and respect the fact that you are using them. Remember, perception, perception, perception, is everything.

Chapter Ten
Count your blessings

I keep talking about balance, and that also means not just having a burning desire to compete with everyone else around you, but it also means counting your current success.

Remember that you have to be happy not just at the end of the journey but all the way through. If you think that you will be happy only when you get to your end goal, you are not being realistic. There is a true story of a couple that kept on upgrading their home. Always arguing with each other, they both firmly believed that once they got to their dream home, they would both be happy. Years went by, and they kept selling and buying until finally they reached their goal home. And as you can guess, they had the worst fight of their marriage in the first night of their dream home. They divorced shortly after. Be happy where you are right now, and remember that someone is worse off than you in the world.

Do you give to charities? You should find one that you really believe in and support it. Even that if it means you only give $5.00 a month, give it. You have to live in a give-and-take world. Only miserable people are self centered.

You will be amazed at how your financial income will improve as you give money to help others. And not to mention the simple fact that you will feel good inside which is important for your overall balanced life.

This will also feed into your ability to not be greedy. The day you start focusing on only your money is the same day you took your eyes off of your goals.

If you focus on only financial gains, then you will not manage your position with success. It is extremely important to not focus on your check-book; it will grow naturally over constant success and steady positional gains.

The real important role for you as an employee is to participate in the events of the corporation. This means birthdays, holidays, and so on. Be a member of the celebration.

If everyone is pitching in $5.00, so should you, and not a dollar more! The worst way out of the office political race is to try to outshine everyone else in your corporation. There is no purpose in advancing you career on broken emotions and relationships; be humble and serve your corporation with honor.

Chapter Eleven

Load your shotgun...

This chapter is about your role as a leader. You must always be present and prepared. Hence, load the shotgun. No one will take you serious if you just walk around with no bullets. Their must be the idea that you are always prepared to pull the trigger when it comes to protecting your position in your corporation. Remember if this is just a paycheck to you, put this book down and pick it back up when you get into your career.

You must be prepared to handle your position and protect your interests in this world. People will respect you if they can take you seriously. That means sacrificing some things you enjoy for a greater cause, perhaps not cracking inappropriate jokes or dressing more the role and less on comfort.

Nothing is handed out to anyone; you got to go get it. Be prepared to fight for the job and protect your hard work. Don't let anyone take credit for your work. It was done with your frame of reference, passion, and input. Claim it!

Remember, cruise control is bad for corporate issues. Never settle down—that is when someone will strike. People must feel that you are serious about your job and take your thoughts as law. Don't use words like *uh, it's like, um,* etc. That is weak, my friend. It sends a message that you are not confident in your place. Get to the point, reword it for clarity, get feedback and move on.

Everyone must know and feel that you are always prepared to defend your thoughts and job. Be firm but open to other ideas and feedback. That way everyone will keep you in on the loop about what activities are going on. Remember the external grapevine?

You may need to one day pull the trigger. Remember to never get upset unless it is in the best interest to preserve your position or protect the company.

Pulling the trigger for any other reason consistently would just turn into a lot of noise all the time, blah, blah, blah.

Chapter Twelve

Put your hand down!

Limitations, we all have them. Stop pretending that you are ready for anything—you are not! Respect your limitations, and you will stay in balance. Going outside of them is trouble.

Remember my words of first just be happy where you are! Then you will make better future advancement goals since you are not focused on negative-based desires like greed or envy. And therefore, you will advance in continuous harmony. Doesn't that sound nice?

The fastest way to fire someone is to promote them, YES! The corporate thought is to take you up the ladder and have you train your replacement, then place you in a position that, YOU ARE NOT ABLE TO HANDLE! Stop thinking you can do everything right regardless of the position and skills needed to do the job right.

Know your limitations. You may just be best as a happy data entry clerk for now. Just be happy.

Regardless of your position, if you are happy in it, you will perform in it, perfect it, and be the highest-earning person in that position. Employers will pay for perfection, and peace of mind. Your joy will also lead to others learning from you, respecting you, and making the corporation a better place. We have tons of angry people—you will stand out.

Again, don't disrespect yourself in thinking you can do more than you're ready for. Keep preparing and be ready. Use your respect that you can't do everything to fuel your pursuit to better yourself. No one in this world is going to push you forward; you must do it.